Pandamoshiums

Readings, Victoria - Pandamoshiums

ISBN 978-1-9996366-1-6

Published in United Kingdom by Victoria Readings

Cover and Interior design and illustrations by Vanessa Medina

To Lily-May, Niall, Kristian, A.K.A The Triplets! You are totally amazing! Thank you for being such wonderful little beings! Kristian, the broccoli page is especially for you and our green lasagne! Love Auntie Vicki xxxx

Hi, I'm Panda!

I'M GOING TO HELP YOU WITH YOUR FEELINGS AND SHOW YOU MAGIC TRICKS YOU CAN DO TO HELP YOU DEAL WITH THEM.

I'M NOT PERFECT, NOBODY IS! THERE ARE THINGS I AM GOOD AT AND THINGS I AM NOT SO GOOD AT.

OUR FEELINGS ALWAYS CHANGE FROM DAY TO DAY,
HOUR BY HOUR, MINUTE TO MINUTE. SOMETIMES
THEY CHANGE IN SECONDS

PANDA CAN BE REALLY HAPPY ONE MINUTE AND THEN REALLY ANGRY OR SAD THE NEXT.

BUT THAT'S OK, OUR FEELINGS ARE PANDEMONIUM...

LET'S EXPLORE SOME OF OUR FEELINGS WITH PANDA...

ANGER

PANDA FEELS ANGRY WHEN SOMEONE DOES SOMETHING HE DOESN'T LIKE OR WHEN OTHERS DO NOT LISTEN TO HIM.

What makes you feel angry?

WHEN PANDA IS ANGRY, IT FEELS LIKE A VOLCANO HAS EXPLODED AND HE STARTS TO SHAKE. HE CLENCHES HIS HANDS AND HE WANTS TO STAMP HIS FEET.
WHAT HAPPENS TO YOUR BODY WHEN YOU ARE ANGRY?

SAD

PANDA FEELS SAD WHEN PEOPLE SAY UNKIND THINGS OR HIS FRIENDS HAVE TO GO HOME AND PANDA HAS TO PLAY ON HIS OWN.

What makes you feel sad?

WHEN PANDA IS SAD HE HAS TEARS RUNNING DOWN HIS FACE AND HE LIKES TO SIT CURLED UP. HIS BODY FEELS HEAVY.

WHAT HAPPENS TO YOUR BODY WHEN YOU FEEL SAD?

SCARED

PANDA CAN FEEL SCARED WHEN IT'S DARK OUTSIDE OR WHEN HE IS IN BED AT NIGHT.

When do you feel scared?

WHEN PANDA FEELS SCARED, HIS TUMMY FEELS FUNNY,
LIKE THERE ARE BUTTERFLIES IN IT AND
HIS BODY SHAKES.

WHAT HAPPENS TO YOUR BODY WHEN YOU FEEL SCARED?

HAPPY

PANDA FEELS HAPPY WHEN HE IS WITH HIS FRIENDS OR AT THE BEACH WITH HIS FAMILY!

What makes you happy?

WHEN PANDA FEELS HAPPY, IT'S LIKE HE IS JUMPING UP IN THE AIR AS HIGH AS HE CAN! HE FEELS GOOD INSIDE AND HAS A SMILE ON HIS FACE!

WHAT DOES YOUR BODY FEEL LIKE WHEN YOU ARE HAPPY?

DISGUST

PANDA DOES NOT LIKE BROCCOLI! YUCK!

What disgusts you? What don't you like?

WHEN PANDA FEELS DISGUSTED, HE POKES HIS
TONGUE OUT AND PULLS A FACE!

WHAT DOES YOUR BODY FEEL LIKE OR DO WHEN YOU ARE
DISGUSTED OR DON'T LIKE SOMETHING?

THESE ARE JUST SOME OF OUR VERY COMPLICATED
EMOTIONS AND FEELINGS!

PANDA HAS FOUR THINGS THAT HELP HIM WITH ALL
OF THESE PANDAMOSHIUMS!

Magic trick number 1

DO SOMETHING YOU ENJOY WHICH MAKES YOU HAPPY!
WHAT IS YOUR FAVOURITE THING TO DO?
WHAT IS YOUR FAVOURITE THING TO EAT?

Magic trick number 2

BREATHE... BREATHE IN THROUGH YOUR NOSE AND OUT THROUGH YOUR MOUTH, HOW DOES YOUR BODY FEEL NOW?

BREATHE IN THROUGH YOUR NOSE...

AND BREATHE OUT THROUGH YOUR MOUTH...

BREATHING HELPS OUR BODIES AND BRAINS FEEL RELAXED!

Magic trick number 3

RELAX AND IMAGINE YOUR FAVOURITE PLACE

Magic trick number 4

WHEN WE MOVE OUR BODIES WE RELEASE HAPPY FEELINGS INSIDE OUR BRAINS WHICH GO THROUGH OUR WHOLE BODY! SO WHY NOT STAR JUMP? SKIP? RIDE YOUR BIKE? DO SOME YOGA? GO SWIMMING? PLAY IN THE GARDEN?

WHAT ELSE CAN YOU THINK OF TO MOVE YOUR BODY AND HELP YOU FEEL HAPPIER?

NOW WE UNDERSTAND SOME OF OUR EMOTIONS AND HAVE SOME MAGIC TRICKS TO HELP US WHEN WE NEED THEM!
POSITIVE
JOYFUL
HAPPY
CONFIDENT

WHERE DO YOU FEEL THESE EMOTIONS IN YOUR BODY?

ANGER
SAD
SCARED
HAPPY
DISGUST

About the Author

Vicki lives in South Wales with her husband and dog! She is originally from the Midlands and has a passion for supporting children in Educational settings and families.

Vicki is a qualified Primary Teacher and loves working with children to develop their creativity, imagination and support their well-being both physical and emotional.
She has trained in a range of techniques to support children and families; Mini Me Yoga, Relax Kids, Baby Mindful and Story Massage.

She has recently trained in a range of Holistic Therapies, offering alternative therapies to people such as Crystal Healing, Angelic Reiki, Indian Head massage, Life Activations and Ensofic Ray.

Vicki is also completing her degree in counselling in Adlerian Counselling.

About the Illustrator

Vanessa (a.k.a. vanesaurus) lives in Padua with her husband and cats. After getting a degree in engineering, her hyperactive right side of the brain took over and decided to leave numbers behind to go chasing unicorns and rainbows. She studied Graphic Arts and also got a degree on Illustration.

She is very passionate about art and beautiful things, and works as a full time freelancer with one (and sometimes, two) cats on her lap and bunny slippers.